WISDOM OF THE EAST

WOMEN AND WISDOM
OF JAPAN

WITH AN INTRODUCTION
BY SHINGORO TAKAISHI

LONDON
JOHN MURRAY, ALBEMARLE STREET
1905

CONTENTS

		PAGE
INTRODUCTION	.	11

I

GIRL'S INSTRUCTION ?. 33

II

DEMARKATION BETWEEN THE SEXES . . . 34

III

"SEVEN REASONS FOR DIVORCE". . . . 35

IV

THE WIFE'S MISCELLANEOUS DUTIES . . . 38

7

8   CONTENTS

V

PAGE

THE TREATMENT OF SERVANTS 42

VI

THE INFIRMITIES OF WOMAN 44

APPENDIX A

THE JAPANESE REVOLUTION 49

APPENDIX B

THE LEGAL CONDITIONS FOR A DIVORCE . . 63

EDITORIAL NOTE

THE object of the editors of this series is a very definite one. They desire above all things that, in their humble way, these books shall be the ambassadors of good-will and understanding between East and West, the old world of Thought, and the new of Action. In this endeavour, and in their own sphere, they are but followers of the highest example in the land. They are confident that a deeper knowledge of the great ideals and lofty philosophy of Oriental thought may help to a revival of that true spirit of Charity which neither despises nor fears the nations of another creed and colour. Finally, in thanking press and public for the very cordial reception given to the "Wisdom of the East" series, they wish to state that no pains have been spared to secure the best specialists for the treatment of the various subjects at hand.

L. CRANMER-BYNG.
S. A. KAPADIA.

THE ORIENT PRESS,
4, HARCOURT BUILDINGS,
INNER TEMPLE,
LONDON.

INTRODUCTION

THE sole basis of the entire moral teaching of Japan may be said, in the briefest phrase, to consist of the spirit of unselfishness. Thus, humility in place of ostentation, reserve in place of *réclame*, self-sacrifice in place of selfishness, forbearance in place of impetuosity, and complete submission to authority are the principal features of the Japanese moral code ; on these corner-stones stands the whole edifice under which the Eastern people have been brought up.

The Onna Daigaku, or the "Greater Learning for Women," which is the text of this little book, is, as its title indicates, a half-dogmatised precept exclusively intended for women. The author is Kaibara Ekken, the famous moralist of Japan, who flourished about two hundred years ago. Kaibara Ekken was a great scholar of Japanese literature, with an immense knowledge of Chinese ethics. It is beyond question that his idea of morality was, to a great extent, formed on Chinese lines, as most of the other thinkers' and moralists'

11

ideas in those days were.   But his style of writing
was by no means the same as that of his compeers.
The tranquillity and uniform peacefulness at-
tained under the Tokugawa Government, thanks
to the subtle and shrewd policy inaugurated by its
revered founder, Iyeyasu, whereby the ambitions
of the great feudal lords had been curbed, had
naturally given a great impetus to the growth
of various arts and of their peaceful pursuance
by the people.   Of the products of that generation literature stood foremost.   The scholars and
thinkers indulged themselves in researches con-
nected with nothing but the higher classics, both
of the Japanese and Chinese.   Their works were
mostly written either in the Chinese way or the
most classical style of their own language, no
matter what were the subjects of their essays.
Amid this pedantic fashion, Kaibara alone busied
himself in expounding his own moral principles
in the most popular style of writing known in
his days.   It is no great wonder that his works
were read by the book-hungered people to such
an extent that in a comparatively short interval
of time it was not seldom that his works were to
be found on even the scantily furnished shelves
in poor merchants' houses, people of a class that
was in those days the least addicted to reading,
save in respect of a few standard books of traditional value and antiquity.

The Onna Daigaku was, of his many books,

the most popular, and for nearly two centuries after its publication it was looked upon throughout the country as one of the indispensable articles of a bride's trousseau box. The general trend of his doctrine, however, was by no means a new one ; there had already been a few similar essays written by typical Samurai moralists dealing with the same subject, though they were of the casual and fragmentary nature. His book, moreover, was certainly not one of those which, as we find here and there in history, have effected great revolutions in the deep-rooted thoughts of a nation or in the moral conceptions prevailing among a people. I believe, nevertheless, that I am not mistaken in describing his book, on the whole, as one which represents and embodies the moral sense of the people of his day. He it was who combined traditional sayings and fragmental precepts with his own morality, and set them down in readable form. Hence, in other words, he guided the masses who had but a vague comprehension of female morality in the direction towards which they wished to be led, and gave them an infallible belief in the truth of his teaching. At the same time it will be well understood that the great demand for his book was due, apart from its own intrinsic merit, to the fact that in those early days there was a ridiculously small number of popular books accessible to the reader, especially for women. Under these circumstances his books had tremendous vogue, and it is indeed hardly to be credited, perhaps, by Western readers how great and sweeping was the influence that the doctrine contained in the Onna Daigaku had upon the popular idea of female morality. It was like a holy command; it was like a religion which people never ventured to depart from nor even to criticise.

It is always a subject for wonder that, apart from the differences that otherwise exist, there should be such utterly opposed ideas existing between Orientals and Occidentals in regard to the moral position of women. While it is undoubtedly a difficult thing to understand, at least for the Easterners, how the Western woman has gained such a pre-eminence over the Western man in social life, it is no less hard for an Occidental to comprehend how the reverse state of things in the East should have come into existence. It seems to me, however, that the old Eastern moralists fully realised the strong influence which the fair sex has ever possessed by her nature over the other sex, and their dread of her resulted in the publication of the doctrine of her subordination to man and of her complete negation as a power. It was as far back as 500 B.C. that Confucius, the greatest of all Chinese teachers, said, " Man and woman should never sit in the same apartment after they reach seven years of age." This was the first principle of

the demarkation of the sexes to be observed
between man and woman, and, indeed, the very
germ of that negativeness of woman with which
the relation between the sexes was to be regarded.
The woman was to be left alone, the man had
nothing to contribute towards her elevation. The
more power the woman had, the stronger were
the wiles against which, they confessed, man
could offer but a feeble resistance. Then there
came another version. The Buddhists said,
"Woman is a creature with the look of an angel
on its countenance, but with a diabolical spirit
in its inmost heart." "Woman is full of sin;
nothing is to be dreaded so much as a woman,"
they further insisted. (It is interesting to note
here that in ancient days this idea was in no way
peculiar to the East, for we know that Socrates
in the West, almost at the same period, said,
"Woman is the source of all evil; her love is to
be dreaded more than the hatred of man; the
poor young men who seek women in matrimony
are like fish who go to meet the hook.")

Thus, as it may be seen, while one school
exhorted men not to have any dealings with
woman, or at least to observe with the utmost
rigidity the line of separation from her, the other
went further, demonstrating her sinfulness and
devilish depravity from the religious point of
view. These ideas, with contemporary civilisation and literature, spread across to Japan from

the Asiatic Continent like eagles in full flight.   It
is no great wonder that in consequence the education of our women was neglected and her in-
telligence became more and more narrow, owing to
there being little or no chance for her to see things
in the outer world.   The next thing which was
bound to happen was man's contempt and disdain
for woman, for her narrow-mindedness and
stupidity.   Thus, one wrong brought another in
its train.

Woman's position in Japan, especially in her
social relations, sank deeper and deeper into
neglect and obscurity, when the incessant
struggles between the feudal lords, generation
after generation, rendered the whole country but
a huge battle-field, and stirred our warriors to
warlike frenzy in their search for the glory of
brave deeds.   This can be fully illustrated when
we remember that some seventeen centuries ago
there was a vague yet indisputable existence of
a kind of Court society, a social feature which
invariably gave ladies excellent chances to raise
their relative influence over courtiers; and that it
was during this age we saw more female writers and
other distinguished members of the fair sex than
ever we did subsequently.   But soon after, when,
what we call Buke Jidai came upon the scene
and the practical hold of the reins shifted from
the Emperor to the Shogun, there was no room
left for woman to display her natural charms.

Everywhere people went they saw nothing but warriors clad in full armour, sword in hand. The Bushi was disappointed and disheartened when he saw his wife gave birth to a girl, because, in his eyes, there was no attainment to rank and fame open to his child in its career : for he could not take her with him to the field, as he could a son, to fight for his lord. Woman became a mere being to rear up the posterity ! Woman was left neglected, became more and more ignorant and docile, and was reduced to a purely domestic existence. It was most disgraceful to a Bushi to be moved by woman's sway, no matter in what directions, or even to think too much of her. A man's heart, it was considered, when occupied with the higher conception of duty and devotion towards the Emperor or his overlord, had no place left for lighter cares. Effeminacy was the most shameful blot upon the chivalry of the age. Though the Bushi was taught to protect the weaker of either sex, yet extreme severity and coolness of demeanour towards the fair sex was regarded as a proof of a man's martial endurance. Truly, as Professor Chamberlain has said, "neither God nor the ladies inspired any enthusiasm in the Samurai's heart," nor did he ever perform his valiant deeds for such a fanciful reward as a lady's smile. Love was understood to be inconsistent with valour : attachment to a woman was feared as a discouragement rather

B

than a stimulant to achievement. Where, then, could the poor woman stand ? But there was no help for it, for it was her fate to submit !

As our readers will see, Kaibara Ekken describes the five worst infirmities which afflict the female mind, and he mentions silliness or stupidity as the worst of all and the parent of the other four. He attributed the inferiority of woman to man more particularly to this fact. It is of importance, in order to understand the true bearing of his doctrine, that this point should be particularly borne in mind. Thus he concludes that when viewed from the standard of man's nature, the foolishness of woman prevents her from understanding the duties that lie before her very eyes. We then have to allow that our women in those days were far inferior to men in every respect than was the case with most of the other races. Blind obedience to her husband, which, he tells us, was the safest way, was considered to have been completely justified by this fact. But I must ask myself what Kaibara meant by the silliness and foolishness of woman. I cannot, however, think that our women, even in those times, were mentally imperfect or lacking in intellect. In short, his point of argument seems to be this : that a woman was too apt to give way to her passion ; as she did not see much of the world, she knew little how to wend her way ; she was too bashful and palpitating of heart to deal wisely with the other sex. Thus a husband was looked upon as a man who is guiding a blind person—one who sees absolutely nothing. It is altogether without significance that so learned a man like Kaibara Ekken did not even attempt to suggest any remedy for females' "foolishness," but that, on the contrary, he took it to be an ineradicable failing due to the nature of the fair sex. Be that as what it may, it is undoubtedly true that the Japanese woman, even at the present day, is the shyest being in the world!

Turning our eyes to the husband—a husband who had such an unrestricted control over his wife and was regarded as the safest guide of his shy and delicate wife—it is most natural that he should at once find himself confronted with important questions. Then, did the Japanese husband fulfil his duty properly in the guidance of his consort? Or, at least, was he well deserving of being entrusted with such a tremendous responsibility? I could not be reproached for a want of straightforwardness if I were to say, answering these questions, that he did not quite deserve to enjoy such warm affection and tender respect as every Japanese wife was willing to pay him. But he was by no means a bad husband. I can say safely that he loved, fondled, and petted his wife, no less than our Western husband does. But the laws of morality forbade him to pay her much respect in the outward manner, and thus to allow her real independence. Here I quite agree with Professor Chamberlain when he rightly and wittily says: "We would not have it thought that Japanese women are actually ill-used; there is probably very little of wife-beating in Japan, neither is there any Zenana system, any veiling of the face; rather is it that women are all their lives treated as babies, neither trusted with the independence which our modern manners allow, nor commanding the romantic homage which was woman's dower in Mediæval Europe." In fact, they were simply petted. The Japanese wife would have been greatly surprised if we should rashly conclude that, inasmuch as she did not share the public enjoyments and pomps of society with her husband, and inasmuch as she did not enjoy the acquaintance of her husband's friends, she was an unhappy wife.

However, apart from all minor considerations, to understand the true significance of the moral sense which gave rise to the Onna Daigaku doctrine, we have to consider the very basis of the general character of moral teaching in Japan. The seeming absurdity and apparent paradox of the doctrine, even to our Eastern eyes, will never be truly understood unless we extend our gaze to the general conception of morality by which the people have so long been governed.

As I said at the beginning, the basis of the
Japanese moral teaching consists in the highest
sense of self-denial, self-abnegation, or any
antithesis to selfishness.   Take for an instance
the Bushido, the most salient feature in the
Japanese morality.   (I may add that there is
no dogma of the Bushido, nor any written code.)
It preaches submission to authority, utter devotion to one's overlord, and self-sacrifice of
all private interest, whether of self or family,
to the common weal.   It is the morale of self-
sacrifice.   Now the Bushido, if it be translated
into English, means "the way of the warriors"
or "warrior's spirit."   In other words, it is a
moral teaching for men; or it may be, for convenience' sake, termed "the Greater learning for
men," compared with "the Greater learning for
women."   Of course, the Bushido is of the more
dominating and overwhelming nature, and covers
a much wider sphere in its application, and,
furthermore, it may be said, almost without any
fear of exaggeration, that the doctrine of Onna
Daigaku is a different form of the Bushido spirit.
This view will be more clearly confirmed when
we notice Kaibara say, "A woman has no particular lord; she must look to her husband."
This is indeed the key of his whole doctrine.
The Bushido commands loyalty to one's lord;
the Onna Daigaku loyalty to woman's husband,
who was, as we have just seen, truly her lord.

Therefore, though it was not inculcated in quite
the same form and manner, we shall see that
what a Bushi did towards his lord was in its
essence what a wife did towards her husband.
The apparent impartiality of her treatment and
severity of duty imposed upon the Japanese
woman by the doctrine was no great wonder
when we, in turn, look upon her husband, who,
under the strictest discipline of the Bushido,
had to act most unselfishly in the discharge of
his duties to his liege lord. So, it is well to be
remembered that the Onna Daigaku is but an
offshoot from the general principle which tells
us that nothing is nobler than self-sacrifice.
Thus we shall also see that it was not woman
only who was to submit to her superior, but so
was man too to his superior, though the objects
of their subjection were not certainly reciprocal.
The moralists of antiquity asked themselves,
" Why should woman alone be freed from the
divine duty of human beings which Nature im-
partially imposed upon us ? " But man of the
present day would retort, " While a man receives
woman's subjection in return for his subjection
to his lord, and thus fills the gap, so to speak ;
where and what can a woman obtain in return
for her subjection to her husband ? " As a man
of the present day I am not backward in joining
my voice to the chorus in this protest.

Next, what we notice is the onerous nature

of duties imposed upon a wife towards her parents-
in-law. This is undoubtedly the outcome of the
combined idea of ancestor-worship and the maintenance of the family name, and also the inevitable
result of the practice of married couples living
in the same house with their parents. An eldest
son, an heir, be he real or adopted, was to
succeed to his father's position as head of the
family; and to make himself a worthy family
head he had to learn every minor matter besides
business affairs, if there were any, appertaining
to the family: from the personality, if not
character, of every member among his relations
—generally numerous in number—and all sorts
of family specialities in various matters, social
or domestic, religious or ceremonial—most of
them descended from the time immemorial—
down to the kinds of gifts to be given to his
tenants and servants on certain occasions; all
had to be well understood by him. His wife,
too, could not be held entirely irresponsible in
these matters. Therefore a man and his wife,
on their wedding, entered into an apprenticeship
under those whom they would presently succeed.
A woman's parents-in-law being, sooner or later,
to join a group of her family ancestors, she was
taught to serve them with the utmost reverence
and worship. We often see even now a large
family where a grandfather and grandmother
enjoy their companionship with their sons and

daughters and boys and girls who are yet further remote offspring of theirs. While solitude and loneliness in a family are with us of rare occurrence, the youthful jubilation of a young couple at their secluded settlement is no usual happening.

Finally, we are naturally anxious to know what effect the doctrine may have brought about upon the Japanese women, or at least how far it has influenced woman's character. The object of the investigation exists now before our eyes, and everybody can draw conclusions as he or she may like. But for my part I am quite certain that for good or evil the Japanese women, to say nothing of the other characters, are the most obedient, docile, submissive, and even most humble women in the world. Thus woman's power of independence and self-reliance so far disappeared, or even if possessed of those qualities, she could hardly find a chance to display them without exciting much objection and disgust in her husband and relatives at large. Of the other characteristics of our women, I am not by any means a good judge, and I think it much better to quote what foreigners—I am glad to say they are chiefly English—say of our women. Professor Chamberlain, who is beyond question an authority on Japan, says, " Japanese women are most womanly, kind, gentle, pretty." Here is a most daring compliment from the pen of an Englishman, which runs as follows : " How

sweet Japanese woman is! All the possibilities
of the race for goodness seem to concentrate in
her. It shakes one's faith in some Oriental
doctrines. If this be the result of suppression
and oppression, then these are not altogether
bad. On the other hand, how diamond-hearted
the character of the American woman becomes
under the idolatry of which she is the object.
In the eternal order of things, which is the higher
being—the childlike, confiding, sweet Japanese
girl, or the superb, calculating, penetrating
Occidental Circe of our more artificial society,
with the enormous power for evil and her limited
capacity for good?" One critic went even
further—little to the comfort of man—saying
decidedly, "They are immeasurably superior
to men." After all this, it is no exaggeration to
say that the unanimous verdict given by Western
observers is, that the Japanese woman is charming, sweet, gentle, and tender. Great compliment
as it is to our women, I am inclined to think that
some judges must have been struck by it as a
strange phenomenon, and, moreover, their conclusions may have been drawn after a little
over-strained experience in their Western matri-
monial life, or some of them may have been prone
to indulge a little in day-dreams.

Yet as a wife, her sincere affection, her loving
tenderness, and her true, faithful devotion to her
husband is most remarkable. It seems to me that

these natures are not merely a "result of suppression and oppression." The late Mr. Lafcadio Hearn, after giving his admirable translation of a diary left by a married Japanese woman, said, "The brave resolve of the woman to win affection by docility and by faultless performance of duty, her gratitude for every small kindness, her childlike piety, her supreme unselfishness, her Buddhist interpretation of suffering as the penalty for some faults committed in a previous life, her attempt to write poetry when her heart was breaking— all this I find touching and more than touching. But I do not find it exceptional! The traits revealed are typical—typical of the moral nature of the people." Indeed, as a wife, the Japanese woman is of a quiet, peaceful disposition, fond of home, virtuous, and generally of an appearance that should not cause her husband to ever be jealous of her. She is homely; haughtiness and superciliousness are foreign to our sense of beauty.

As for an unmarried girl, men might almost say, "We don't know what she is like." She is not the property of any young man, nor does she belong to herself, but to her parents. Friendship between a girl and a young man is nonexistent in Japan. A girl at present is not at all under such a strict supervision as she was in former days, yet she is incapable of meeting young men on terms of equality, even to have a two minutes' talk with them ; she is more than shy, bashful, and palpitating. She does not, on the other hand, appear in man's eyes anything but a delicate and fragile porcelain figure. Of course, man is not quite free from censure, since his handling of the figure is not altogether gentle. Marriage being carried out entirely by her parents' will, her virgin days form but a long continuation of her child life ; of flirtation and courtship she knows nothing. One may, then, naturally wonder what a dull life a Japanese young man leads !

Lastly, I may briefly touch upon the present state of the problem. As things in Japan are still in a state of transition after such a great social revolution,* and especially so of the people's morals, it is no easy task to see in which direction the wind is really blowing. At present, however, the people have not to any noticeable extent departed from the spirit resting upon Kaibara's doctrine. Of course, I must mention that his work, the Onna Daigaku, is no longer a favourite book of women, and that perhaps nine girls out of ten have not had even a glimpse of its famous pages. But as the Onna Daigaku was, as I said before, an embodiment of the people's moral nature, the important meaning of the doctrine, needless to say, does not rest upon the book, but upon the heads of the people

* See the Appendix A.

themselves, and so far the people have not undergone much change in their mode of thought with
regard to this problem. Hence text-books in
girls' schools are more or less imbued with the
doctrine in the original or in a modified form.
There was, however, an attempt to overthrow
the prevailing idea by the late Mr. Fukuzawa,
the greatest educator of modern Japan, to whom
present Japan owes much of its civilisation,
which culminated in the promulgation of the
Shin Onna Daigaku or " the new greater learning
for women." Great and formidable as his success
was in the other departments of thought, his
new effort has not, up to the present, brought
about much important effect upon the problem.
So long as, I think, the present family system of
the people and their customs and condition of
living do not make any marked change, a comparatively large portion of the doctrine will hold
good and be found convenient by men. But on
the other hand, if women in new Japan become
more enlightened and look for happiness, both
for men and women, in a new form, and start
themselves a movement for the " emancipation
of women," how things will turn out I cannot
say. But I can, at the same time, assure our
women that there is an unexpectedly large number
of men who are quite ready to back them up if
any of those movements should come to the fore.
To avoid any possible misunderstanding on

the part of my readers, I feel it my duty to add here that with regard to the severance of conjugal relations between a husband and wife, the reasons minutely enumerated by Kaibara have no importance whatever, and these matters are now distinctly regulated by the Civil Code, an extract of which will be found at the end of the book.

SHINGORO TAKAISHI.

April, 1905.

たかいし しんごぼ

WOMEN AND WISDOM
OF JAPAN

I

GIRL'S INSTRUCTION

SEEING that it is a girl's destiny, on reaching
womanhood, to go to a new home, and live
in submission to her father-in-law, it is even more
incumbent upon her than it is on a boy to receive
with all reverence her parents' instructions.
Should her parents, through her tenderness, allow
her to grow up self-willed, she will infallibly show
herself capricious in her husband's house, and
thus alienate his affection; while, if her father-
in-law be a man of correct principles, the girl
will find the yoke of these principles intolerable.
She will hate and decry her father-in-law, and
the end of these domestic dissensions will be her
dismissal from her husband's house and the
covering of herself with ignominy. Her parents,
forgetting the faulty education they gave her,
may, indeed, lay all the blame on the father-in-
law. But they will be in error; for the whole
disaster should rightly be attributed to the faulty
education the girl received from her parents.

More precious in a woman is a virtuous heart

than a face of beauty. The vicious woman's heart is ever excited ; she glares wildly around her, she vents her anger on others, her words are harsh and her accent vulgar. When she speaks, it is to set herself above others, to upbraid others, to envy others, to be puffed up with individual pride, to jeer at others, to outdo others—all things at variance with the way in which a woman should walk. The only qualities that befit a woman are gentle obedience, chastity, mercy, and quietness.

II

DEMARKATION BETWEEN THE SEXES

FROM her earliest youth a girl should observe the line of demarkation separating women from men, and never, even for an instant, should she be allowed to see or hear the least impropriety. The customs of antiquity did not allow men and women to sit in the same apartment, to keep their wearing apparel in the same place, to bathe in the same place, or to transmit to each other anything directly from hand to hand. A woman going abroad at night must in all cases carry a lighted lamp ; and (not to speak of strangers) she must observe a certain distance in her relations even with her husband and with her brothers. In our days the women of lower classes, ignoring all rules of this nature, behave themselves disorderly; they contaminate their reputations, bring down reproach upon the head of their parents and brothers, and spend their whole lives in an unprofitable manner. Is not this truly lamentable? It is written likewise in the *Lesser Learning* that a woman must form no friendship and no intimacy except when ordered to do so by her parents or by middlemen.[1] Even at the peril of her life must she harden her heart like rock or metal and observe the rules of propriety.

. . . . . .

III

" SEVEN REASONS FOR DIVORCE "

IN China marriage is called "returning," for the reason that a woman must consider her husband's home as her own, and that, when she marries, she is therefore returning to her own home. However low and needy her husband's position may be, she must find no fault with him, but consider the poverty of the household which

---

[1] The middleman is the go-between. It is the parents' duty in Japan to secure a suitable partner for their child, and, in turn, the conduct of the affair is customarily intrusted to a third person (generally some married friend of theirs). The middleman thus negotiates the marriage, and often remains through life a sort of godfather to the young couple.

it has pleased Heaven to give her as the ordering of an unpropitious fate. The sage of old taught that, once married, she must never leave her husband's house. Should she forsake the " way " and be divorced, shame shall cover her till her latest hour. With regard to this point, there are seven faults which are termed the " Seven Reasons for Divorce " : [1]

(i) A woman shall be divorced for disobedience to her father-in-law or mother-in-law. (ii) A woman shall be divorced if she fail to bear children, the reason for this rule being that women are sought in marriage for the purpose of giving men posterity. A barren woman should, however, be retained if her heart be virtuous and her conduct correct and free from jealousy, in which case a child of the same blood must be adopted ; neither is there any just cause for a man to divorce a barren wife if he have children by a concubine. (iii) Lewdness is a reason for divorce. (iv) Jealousy is a reason for divorce. (v) Leprosy or any like foul disease is a reason for divorce. (vi) A woman shall be divorced who, by

[1] Before the present system of government was adopted—that is to say, about forty years ago—Japan had no divorce law, nor a court for such a petition, and the divorce was effected either by mutual agreement between the husband and wife or entirely by the husband's will. As any of these reasons was justifiable for a husband to announce a divorce against his wife, the reasons enumerated here, in a sense, appeared to have amounted to a code of law. For the present condition see the Appendix B.

talking overmuch and prattling disrespectfully, disturbs the harmony of kinsmen and brings trouble on her household.   (vii) A woman shall be divorced who is addicted to stealing.   All the "Seven Reasons for Divorce" were taught by the sage.   A woman, once married, and then divorced, has wandered from the "way," and is covered with great shame, even if she should enter into a second union with a man of wealth and position.

It is the chief duty of a girl living in the parental house to practise filial piety towards her father and mother.   But after marriage her duty is to honour her father-in-law and mother-in-law, to honour them beyond her father and mother, to love and reverence them with all ardour, and to tend them with practice of every filial piety.   While thou honourest thine own parents, think not lightly of thy father-in-law !   Never should a woman fail, night and morning, to pay her respects to her father-in-law and mother-in-law.   Never should she be remiss in performing any tasks they may require of her.   With all reverence must she carry out, and never rebel against, her father-in-law's commands.   On every point must she inquire of her father-in-law and mother-in-law, and abandon herself to their direction.   Even if thy father-in-law and mother-in-law be pleased to hate and vilify thee, be not

angry with them, and murmur not. If thou
carry piety towards them to its utmost limits,
and minister to them in all sincerity, it cannot
be but that they will end by becoming friendly
to thee.

IV

THE WIFE'S MISCELLANEOUS DUTIES

A ·WOMAN has no particular lord. She must
look to her husband as her lord, and must serve
him with all worship and reverence, not despising
or thinking lightly of him. The great lifelong
duty of a woman is obedience. In her dealings
with her husband, both the expression of her
countenance and style of her address should be
courteous, humble, and conciliatory, never peevish
and intractable, never rude and arrogant—that
should be a woman's first and chiefest care.
When the husband issues his instructions, the
wife must never disobey them. In doubtful
case she should inquire of her husband, and
obediently follow his commands. If ever her
husband should inquire of her, she should answer
to the point—to answer in a careless fashion were
a mark of rudeness. Should her husband be
roused at any time to anger, she must obey him
with fear and trembling, and not set herself up
against him in anger and forwardness. A woman

should look on her husband as if he were Heaven itself, and never weary of thinking how she may yield to her husband and thus escape celestial castigation.

As brothers-in-law and sisters-in-law are the brothers and sisters of a woman's husband, they deserve all her reverence. Should she lay herself open to the ridicule and dislike of her husband's kindred, she would offend her parents-in-law, and do harm even to herself; whereas, if she lives on good terms with them, she will likewise rejoice the hearts of parents-in-law. Again, she should cherish, and be intimate with, her brother-in-law and his wife, esteeming them as she does her own elder brother and sister.

Let her never even dream of jealousy. If her husband be dissolute, she must expostulate with him, but never either nurse or vent her anger. If her jealousy be extreme, it will render her countenance frightful and her accent repulsive, and can only result in completely alienating her husband from her, and making her intolerable to his eyes. Should her husband act ill and unreasonably, she must compose her countenance and soften her voice to remonstrate with him; and if he be angry and listen not to the remonstrance, she must wait over a season, and then expostulate with him again when his heart is softened. Never set thyself up against thy husband with harsh features and a boisterous voice.

.   .   .   .   .

A woman should be circumspect and sparing in her use of words, and never, even for a passing moment, should she slander others or be guilty of untruthfulness. Should she ever hear of calumny, she should keep it to herself and repeat it to none; for it is retailing of calumny that disturbs the harmony of kinsmen and ruins the peace of families.

.   .   .   .   .

A woman must be ever on the alert, and keep a strict watch over her own conduct. In the morning she must rise early, and at night go late to rest. Instead of sleeping in the middle of the day, she must be intent on the duties of her household, and must not weary of weaving, sewing, and spinning. Of tea and wine she must not drink overmuch, nor must she feed her eyes and ears with theatrical performances, ditties, and ballads. To temples [1] (whether Shinto or Buddhist) and other like places where there is a great concourse of people, she should go but sparingly till she has reached the age of forty.

.   .   .   .   .

[1] The Japanese temples are the centres of festivals, and people go there not only for worshipping, but pleasure; indeed, a great number for the latter purpose. The Scotch game or market-day in the country may be likened to the turn-out of these occasions.

She must not let herself be led astray by
mediums and divineresses, and enter into an
irreverent familiarity with the gods; neither
should she be constantly occupied in praying.
If only she satisfactorily perform her duties as
a human being, she may let prayer alone without
ceasing to enjoy the divine protection.

In her capacity of wife, she must keep her
husband's household in proper order. If the
wife be evil and profligate, the house is ruined.
In everything she must avoid extravagance, and
both with regard to food and raiment must act
according to her station in life, and never give
way to luxury and pride.

While young, she must avoid the intimacy
and familiarity of her husband's kinsmen, com-
rades, and retainers, ever strictly adhering to
the rule of separation between the sexes; and
on no account whatever should she enter into
correspondence with a young man. Her personal
adornments and the colour and pattern of her
garments should be unobtrusive. It suffices for
her to be neat and cleanly in her person and in
her wearing apparel. It is wrong in her, by an
excess of care, to obtrude herself on other people's
notice. Only that which is suitable should be
practised.

She must not selfishly think first of her own

parents and only secondly of her husband's relations. At New Year, on Five Festivals, and on other like occasions she should pay her first respect to those of her husband's house, and then to her own parents. Without her husband's permission, she must go nowhere, neither should she make any gift on her own responsibility.

.   .   .   .   .

As a woman rears up posterity not to her own parents, but to her father-in-law and mother-in-law, she must value the latter even more than the former, and tend them filial piety. Her visits, also, to the paternal house should be rare after marriage. Much more then with regard to other friends should it generally suffice for her to send a message to inquire after their health. Again, she must not be filled with pride at the recollection of the splendour of her parental house, and must not make it the subject of her conversations.

.   .   .   .   .

V

THE TREATMENT OF SERVANTS

HOWEVER many servants she may have in her employ, it is a woman's duty not to shirk the

¹ The Japanese parlourmaids are more concerned with the household in which they are employed, and more familiar to their masters, mistresses, and other members of the family than the English ones.

trouble of attending to everything herself. She must sew her father-in-law's and mother-in-law's garments, and make ready their food. Ever attentive to the requirements of her husband, she must fold his clothes and dust his rug, rear his children, wash what is dirty, be constantly in the midst of her household, and never go abroad but of necessity.

.   .   .   .

Her treatment of her handmaidens will require circumspection. Those low-born girls have had no proper education; they are stupid, obstinate, and vulgar in their speech. When anything in the conduct of their mistress's husband or parents-in-law crosses their wishes, they fill her ears with their invectives, thinking thereby to render her a service. But any woman who should listen to this gossip must beware of the heart-burnings it will be sure to breed. Easy is it by reproaches and disobedience to lose the love of those who, like a woman's marriage connections, were all originally strangers ; and it were surely folly, by believing the prattle of a servant-girl, to diminish the affection of a precious father-in-law and mother-in-law. If a servant girl be altogether too loquacious and bad, she should speedily be dismissed ; for it is by the gossips of such persons that occasion is given for the troubling of the harmony of kinsmen and the disordering of a household. Again, in her dealings with these low people, a woman will find many things to disapprove of. But if she be for ever reproving and scolding, and spend her time in hustle and anger, her household will be in a continual state of disturbance. When there is real wrongdoing, she should occasionally notice it, and point out the path of amendment, while lesser faults should be quietly endured without anger. While in her heart she compassionates her subordinates' weakness, she must outwardly admonish them with all strictness to walk in the path of propriety, and never allow them to fall into idleness. If any is to be succoured, let her not be grudging of her money ; but she must not foolishly shower down her gifts on such as merely please her individual caprice, but are unprofitable servants.

.   .   .   .   .

VI

THE INFIRMITIES OF WOMAN

THE five worst infirmities that afflict the female are indocility, discontent, slander, jealousy, and silliness. Without any doubt, these five infirmities are found in seven or eight out of every ten women, and it is from these that arises the inferiority of women to men. A woman should cure them by self-inspection and self-reproach.

The worst of them all and the parent of the other four is silliness. Woman's nature is passive. This passiveness being of the nature of night is dark. Hence, as viewed from the standard of man's nature, the foolishness of woman fails to understand the duties that lie before her very eyes, perceives not the actions that will bring down blame upon her own head, and comprehends not even the things that will bring down calamities on the head of her husband and children. Neither when she blames and accuses and curses innocent persons, nor when, in her jealousy of others, she thinks to set up herself alone, does she see that she is her own enemy, estranging others and incurring their hatred. Lamentable errors! Again, in the education of her children, her blind affection induces an erroneous system. Such is the stupidity of her character that it is incumbent on her, in every particular, to distrust herself and to obey her husband.

We are told that it was the custom of the ancients, on the birth of a female child, to let it lie on the floor for the space of three days. Even in this may be seen the likening of the man to heaven and of the woman to earth; and the custom should teach a woman how necessary it is for her in everything to yield to her husband the first, and to be herself content with the second place; to avoid pride, even if there be in her

actions aught deserving praise ; and, on the other
hand, if she transgress in aught and incur blame,
to wend her way through the difficulty and amend
the fault, and so conduct herself as not again to
lay herself open to censure ; to endure without
anger and indignation the jeers of others, suffering
such things with patience and humility. If a
woman acts thus, her conjugal relation cannot
but be harmonious and enduring, and her household a scene of peace and concord.

.   .   .   .   .

Parents ! teach the foregoing maxims to your
daughters from their tenderest years ! Copy
them out from time to time, that they may read
and never forget them ! Better than the garments and divers vessels which the fathers of
the present day so lavishly bestow upon their
daughters when giving them away in marriage,
were it to teach them thoroughly these precepts,
which would guard them as a precious jewel
throughout their lives. How true is that ancient
saying : " A man knoweth how to spend a million
pieces of money in marrying off his daughter,
but knoweth not how to spend a hundred thou-
sand in bringing up his child ! " Such as have
daughters must lay this well to heart.

APPENDICES

APPENDIX A

THE JAPANESE REVOLUTION

EVERY historian who deals with the modern history of Japan dates the new epoch from the time when the American Commodore Perry came to this country with his "black ships," as the Japanese then called warships.

I cannot venture to depart from this established precedent in my description, and, indeed, using a favourite Japanese phrase, the blank shot fired from Perry's ships was the signal for the raising of the curtain which had covered the whole country, and behind which the people had revelled in their entire isolation from the outer world for so many years.

Now it was in 1853 when Perry paid his armed yet very peaceful visit to this hermit country. It was only some months ago that the fiftieth anniversary of his visit was celebrated at Tokio with a full expression of the national gratitude to him and his country.

Well, I think it is important to give you here

some idea as to the condition of the country at
this time. Japan was then under the Government
of the Tokugawa Shyogun ; that is to say, the
inhabitants dwelt under a feudal system which
had been so carefully planned by the founder of
the Tokugawa Dynasty that his line lasted for
the longest period that ever the feudal rulers in
Japan enjoyed, *viz.* 260 years.

I have to explain what the Shyogun's position
really was. The Shyogun was the Emperor's
deputy. The principle of the relationship between him and the Emperor (known in Europe
as the Mikado) was never put down in any statute,
but practically it was very simple and clear,
because, frankly speaking, such power as the
Shyogun then enjoyed had really been wrested
from the Emperor, though it was obtained by
peaceful methods, and was justified by time-
honoured traditions. It was, as a matter of fact,
announced by the Shyogun that he was entrusted
by the Emperor with the whole affairs of the
State, the Emperor reserving no power of sanction
or veto with regard to his conduct. In short, the
Emperor gave up all those rights and duties
which properly attach to the Sovereign of a
country except the actual occupancy of the
throne. The Shyogun might declare war against
a foreign country, as well as make a treaty with
one, without sanction from the Emperor, and
might even ignore him altogether as regards the

negotiations. This is a brief statement of their relationship.

The Shyogun resided in Yedo (now Tokio) with all his Governmental officials, and the Emperor dwelt in Kyoto. Yedo of course took the shape of a capital, with the largest population, wealth, luxury, and social prosperity. Under the Shyogun there were about 300 Daimyo, *i.e.* feudal lords, each possessing subjects and lands in his own locality.

As to the diplomacy of the country the motto of the founder of the Tokugawa Dynasty was "no intercourse whatever." This would have been beyond question the best way to keep the nation uninformed and undisturbed, and therefore prepared to give blind obedience to the Shyogun. There were but few in those days who knew that there was a vast land called America, or were cognisant of the existence of Great Britain.

In these circumstances it is hardly possible to imagine now how great the wonder was when they knew of the sudden presence of the American ships near Yedo Bay. The whole nation felt that it had lost its individuality. The people had no idea of friendly intercourse between nations. The existence of a State was deemed to be at an end when it came into contact with some superior State. The maintenance of a State in friendly intercourse with another was looked upon as a matter of impossibility. "The weaker," it was supposed, " always went to the wall."

Let me now come back to the subject of the " black ships."   While the event created such an astonishment and alarm throughout the country as had never been known before, it served as a stimulant to the people's mind, as well as pointed out a path leading to the downfall of the Toku-gawa Government. Finding the task of dealing with the Americans too onerous for its own capacity, or considering the responsibility for the affairs to be altogether too great, the Yedo Government made a new departure from its long-cherished governing principle. It summoned the feudal lords to consider, firstly the course that should be pursued, and secondly to prepare an address to the Court in Kioto—that is to say, to the Emperor—a formal report concerning the advent of the American ships. Never pre-viously had the Yedo Government asked the feudal lords for their opinions as such, nor had it officially acquainted the Emperor with affairs of State. It is important to notice that this very act constituted a fatal blow to the Shyogun's administration, inasmuch as it was an open abrogation of its thereunto unique and autocratic authority.

Let us now see what was the general attitude towards this momentous question of opening the country. Needless to say, the largest section of

the people was dead against conceding anything
to the aliens. They had no reasons to urge for
their conviction, but they regarded the isolation
of the country as a divinely inherited creed, and
therefore they did not want to reason about it,
but simply to believe in it. Yet I may divide the
people into three parties for convenience' sake.
The members of the first were what we then called
"Dutch Students," who advocated the opening
of the country, and maintained very liberal and
progressive views.

Judging from their argument, their opinion was
quite in accord with Free Trade. But this section,
of course, was numerically small, and had no
influence upon the public at that early date.
The second consisted of the people, who were
also anti-foreign, but insisted on temporary com-
pliance with the aliens' wishes, hoping to gain
time to develop the national strength, so that
they could presently beat off the foreign intruders.
This opinion was held by comparatively a large
number of educated people, and no doubt the
Yedo Government was largely inspired by this
policy.

Meanwhile, Commodore Perry, who had left the
country the previous year under a promise that
the Yedo Government would give a definite answer
in the following year, now came over once more
to repeat the tactics he had employed before.
After a long and embarrassing council, the Yedo

Government at last found no other course but to open some comparatively unimportant ports in 1858.

This concession, I may say, was the signal for an outburst of national indignation. By this time the doctrine to revere the Emperor, which was renewed and emphasised some half century before by Shinto scholars and many profound thinkers, had now begun to bear fruit in the minds of a large section of the people. Disgusted with the Yedo Government, which, they thought, had disgracefully given way to the foreigners, and inspired by the doctrine of the superiority of the Emperor, the whole nation closed up into one party to resist this national calamity. The cry of "Son-no-jo-i" was reverberated from end to end of the country. "Son-no-jo-i" means, "Revere the sovereign, expel the aliens." Thus the first act of the revolution was opened.

The dispute as regards the opening of the country had by this time been dropped and put into the background. The most important question was this : how to elect a powerful Government to deal with the national affairs in accordance with their ancestral dignity. No doubt this idea began to take root in the people's mind, owing to the revelation of the weakness of the Yedo Government.

Unfortunately for the Shyogun's Government, amidst this controversy they lost the services of their ablest premier, Tairo Ii, who was assassinated by a band of the Mito Clan's Samurai, who were indignant at his high-handed policy in oppressing the antagonists to the Yedo administration. After his death the Shyogun was practically unable to control his subjects, and for the moment the country seemed to be in a state of complete anarchy, and a large number of the feudal lords knew not what to do.

To solve the momentous question how to elect an effective Government, there was first put forward a moderate doctrine entitled a "System of Co-operative Government." Its principal feature was to bring both the Emperor and Shyogun into a workable Government. This opinion was held by many responsible and powerful feudal lords, as well as by a great number of their able subjects, and it was most popular and therefore had great influence, because the largest portion of the feudal lords and people were as well devoted and loyal to their feudal ruler the Shyogun as to the Emperor, and even the radical party, it seems to me, never thought at the beginning of such a complete destruction of the Shyogun's Government as they devised later on.

However, to understand the situation it must be remembered that there was a peculiar section of people who had never paid homage to the Shyogun and had the easiest access to the Emperor. They were what we called "Kuge"

—the Court nobility. They were the descendants of the nobility, who once exerted great influence in the Court when the Emperor had personally governed the country. While the reins were in the hands of the Shyogun they had nothing to do but to attend some occasional Court ceremonials, and practically had no influence either politically or socially. But now this group of nobility began to play a most important part in the drama of the revolution. Furthermore, it happened that there were some clever and statesmanlike politicians among them.

Quite naturally the majority of the nobility did not like the principle of " give and take," that is, of " Co-operative Government," but aimed at the perfect restoration of power to the Kyoto Court. At this time a number of young and ambitious Samurai, of comparatively low rank, under their respective lords, were gravitating towards the Kyoto Court, and there found friends among the nobility. The Samurai of the Chyoshyu Clan, one of the most powerful, at last persuaded their lord to take most decisive measures to support the Kyoto Court in an effort to regain power. The Court nobility thus brought a most powerful chieftain to their aid. By this time the Satsuma Clan, also one of the strongest, was changing its opinion in favour of the support of the Kyoto policy, and therefore formed an alliance with the Chyoshyu Clan, against whom a little time before they had fought a fight for the Shyogun. Consequently, although the intrigue of the nobility with Chyoshyu to overturn the Yedo Government had been foiled on account of its premature disclosure, yet when the Shyogun sent troops to attack Chyoshyu, he found that the Satsuma's Samurai were acting upon a secret understanding with the objects of his wrath.

On the whole, however, the overthrow of the Yedo Government and the restoration of the Kyoto Court was not yet a popular course. In addition to this, the Emperor Komei, father of the present Emperor, himself did not wish such a radical change of the Government, and the moderate nobility also supported the policy of " co-operation." Therefore, when the Chyoshyu's intrigue was discovered, the Emperor dismissed the nobility who took part in the matter, and they thus forfeited their titles.

In spite of this general desire for a peaceful and amicable settlement, there was an irresistible adverse current running underneath the whole surface. By this time the new Shyogun Keiki found more acutely than before that he was standing in a more and more difficult position, and that the ancient power of Shyogun had now vanished. This was a quite natural and necessary result of their action, because, as I have said before, the Yedo Government had already departed from its well-planned and fundamental

principle, which had its backbone in feudalism.
Consequently, after the Shyogun's self-effacing
act, the Yedo Government, although it retained
to some extent its shape, may be likened to a
body of which the spiritual essence has departed.

At this time the chief of Tosa, a clan no less
important than Satsuma or Chyoshyu, presented
a remarkable memorial to the new Shyogun
Keiki, setting forth the helplessness of the Yedo
Government, and urging that in the interest of
good Government, and in order that the nation's
united strength might be available to meet the
contingencies of its new career, the administrative
power should be restored to the Emperor. Beyond
question it must have been ridiculous to listen
to such a plea if the Shyogun's power had re-
mained unchanged. But Keiki himself was a
man of common sense and loyal to the Emperor.
No doubt he was convinced that the Shyogun's
power had already gone for ever, and to attempt
to keep up its old prestige was tantamount to
awaiting the forced destruction of its whole
edifice by other hands, and that, if it was once
done, the glorious family of Tokugawa might
have been completely effaced from contemporary
history. Thus Tosa's timely advice gave definite
form to his convictions, and at last, in 1867,
fourteen years after the American advent to the
country, the Shyogun Tokugawa Keiki presented
a formal address to the present Emperor to be

permitted to give up his administrative powers
into the Sovereign's own hands.   It was a great
as well as patriotic determination on the part of
Keiki, and well worthy the admiration of his
compatriots, in that he gave up for his country
his Court at Yedo, which had lacked no attribute
of stately magnificence or autocratic strength,
and retired wholly into private life.   Nevertheless,
this pacific act of the Shyogun was not received
with much sympathy by some of the nobility
and by the Samurai from the Satsuma and
Chyoshyu Clans, who were now the best friends
of the nobility.   On the contrary, they desired
not only to exclude the Shyogun Keiki from
taking part in the new Government, but decided
to ask him to abandon his fief and people at once.
Apparently the chasm between the Revolutionists,
or, I may say, the Imperialists, and the Shyogun
was absolutely unbridgeable.   The Imperialists
had in view the thorough abrogation of the Shyogun's office and the creation of a strong central
Government under direct control of the Emperor.
In the face of such provocation Keiki, greatly
moved by his loyal vassals, took up arms against
Kyoto.   But his force was defeated at the beginning by the Samurai of the southern clans,
and he retired to Yedo (now Tokio), the seat of
his Court, about three hundred miles north-east
of Kyoto.
   Thereupon a regular army was formed at Kyoto

under the name of the "Imperial Army," to attack Yedo; but when the force came near Yedo, the sensible Shyogun still did not lose his judgment, and evinced his appreciation of the situation in declaring once more his willingness to hand over his capital and to give up all his power. It will be remembered, although he voluntarily surrendered, he had still the majority of the feudal lords with him, and, if he had so desired, he could have accumulated a strong force, more powerful even than the Imperial Army.

In spite of his determined surrender, his vassals in Yedo, and the clans' Samuria in several localities armed themselves, at their own discretion, against the Imperialists, and fought for their cause with the most admirable sincerity and daring. Nevertheless, the Shyogunites, some of whom made so stubborn a resistance that they went to Yezo or Hokkaido, the extreme north of the country, and there proclaimed the establishment of a republic, were at last defeated and surrendered. I may add that Viscount Hayashi, the present Japanese Minister at the Court of St. James, was one of the Royal Shyogunites, and fought till the last, when he and his colleagues surrendered to the Imperial Army at a besieged fort in Hokkaido.

Thus universal tranquillity was at last gained after one-and-a-half year's unrest, dating from

the time that the Shyogun formally restored his
power.

What I have said is only a very broad outline
of how the Japanese Revolution was carried out.
In conclusion I must now briefly refer to the
effects which it had upon the general policy of
the country. I think you all understand the
revolution was prompted by an inspiration to
expel the aliens and in reverence for the sovereign, and that therefore the new Government
was the product of this anti-foreign idea. However, the scene had undergone a sudden change;
anti-foreignism had vanished altogether. The
new Government hastened to introduce the
Western civilisation as much as they could.
Everything of Japanese native production was
now contemptuously put aside as "old and
obsolete." More and more the Government
sent students in numbers to every country where
they thought they could learn Western civilisation. The people who were not very long ago
fiercely angry with everything foreign, now did
not witness these changes with any sense of
surprise whatever. They joined triumphantly
in the new policy of the new Government. While
respect for antiquity vanished, newness was the
very mainspring and life of everything. This
peculiar state of things is explained in two ways.
First, the cry of "Alien expulsion" was raised
mainly to condemn the policy of the Shyogun's

Government, and thus to make the movement against Yedo appear a legitimate one. Secondly, the people got to know more about the foreigners after the opening of the country, which the Tokugawa Government was forced to do by the American envoy, and, seeing their superiority as well as their peaceful motives, they now fully recognised the advantages of maintaining the policy of the open door and of accommodating themselves to Western civilisation, and assimilating its advantages.

Finally, in the year 23 Meiji, that is to say, about fifteen years ago from the present date, the new constitution which set forth the principle of the limited monarchy, having more resemblance to the British than any other country's, was promulgated, and the new Cabinet under the new constitution was formed with the Premier Marquis Ito, who was one of the Chyoshyu's Samurai.

APPENDIX B

THE LEGAL CONDITIONS FOR A DIVORCE

An Extract from the Japanese Civil Code

Prov. 808. The husband and wife may effect a divorce by mutual consent.

Prov. 809. A person who has not reached the age of twenty-five in order to effect a divorce by mutual consent must obtain the consent of those persons whose consent, according to Arts. 772 and 773, would be necessary to his contracting a marriage.

Prov. 813 (judicial divorce). A husband or a wife, as the case may be, can bring an action for divorce only in the following cases :

1. If the other party contracts a second marriage.
2. If the wife commits adultery.
3. If the husband is sentenced to punishment for an offence involving criminal carnal intercourse.
4. If the other party is sentenced to punishment for an offence greater than misdemeanour, involving forgery, bribery,

sexual immorality, theft, robbery, obtaining property by false pretences, embezzlement of goods deposited, receiving property obtained criminally, or any of the offences specified in Arts. 175 or 260 of the Criminal Code, or is sentenced to a major imprisonment or more.

5. If any party is deserted by the other with wilful intention.

6. If any party is ill-treated or grossly insulted by an ascendant of the other party.

7. If an ascendant of one party is ill-treated or grossly insulted by the other party.

8. If it has been uncertain for three years or more whether the other party was alive or dead.

9. In the case of the adoption of a Mukoyoshi,[1] if the adoption is dissolved ; or in the case of the marriage of an adopted son with a daughter of the house, if the adoption is dissolved or cancelled.

[1] Mukoyoshi is a person who is adopted by another, and at the same time marries the daughter of the house, who would be the heir to the headship of the house.

Printed by Hazell, Watson & Viney, Ld., London and Aylesbury.

THE

WISDOM OF THE EAST SERIES

Edited by L. CRANMER-BYNG and Dr. S. A. KAPADIA

THE object of the Editors of this Series is a very definite one They desire above all things that, in their humble way, these books shall be the ambassadors of good-will and understanding between East and West, the old world of Thought and the new of Action. In this endeavour, and in their own sphere, they are but followers of the highest example in the land. They are confident that a deeper knowledge of the great ideals and lofty philosophy of Oriental thought may help to a revival of that true spirit of Charity which neither despises nor fears the nations of another creed and colour. Finally, in thanking press and public for the very cordial reception given to the "Wisdom of the East" Series, they wish to state that no pains have been spared to secure the best specialists for the treatment of the various subjects at hand.

LONDON
JOHN MURRAY, ALBEMARLE STREET, W.

EXTRACTS FROM A FEW PRESS OPINIONS

The Athenæum.—"We wish that there were more of them; they are dreamy, lifelike, and fascinating."

St. James's Gazette.—"The quaint and picturesque little 'Wisdom of the East' Series."

Pall Mall Gazette.—"No translation of this important work has been made since the beginning of the eighteenth century."

The Academy.—"Slim, tastefully bound little volumes."

Manchester Courier.—"Worthy of close study by all who would penetrate to the depth of Eastern thought and feeling."

Literary Guide.—"We wish success to this little series of books."

Outlook.—"This Series is published to help in the process of renewing the spiritual and moral life of the West."

The Scotsman.—"This Series should not fail to please readers of the more studious sort."

Nottingham Press.—"This dainty little Volume is the fifth of the Series, all the Earlier Volumes of which have been cordially welcomed by Press and Public alike."

Southport Guardian.—"This Series will find considerable favour with all Students of Eastern Literature and Eastern Philosophy."

The Northern Weekly.—"I must confess that I am attracted by the Literature of the East. This week I have been reading the dainty little books issued by the Orient Press."

Bristol Mercury.—"We commend these little books to all who imagine that there is no knowledge worth having outside Europe and America."

Glasgow Herald.—"This new Series has a definite and lofty aim, and is deserving of support. The books are small, cheap, and well adapted for the pocket. Every page is regularly refreshing and stimulating."

North Devon Journal.—"The difference between Eastern and Western modes of thought is pointedly exemplified by this Series."

Halifax Guardian.—"They are well worth perusal and are presented to the reader in that attractive form which the Orient Press has been happy enough to hit on."

Jewish Chronicle.—"No such near approach to an English translation has ever been made."

Christian Age.—"Meditation on the teaching of this little book cannot but be helpful to all its readers."

Field.—"Such books are valuable aids to the understanding of a far-off age and people, and have a great interest for the student of literature."

Irish Times.—"The volumes are charming in form, low in price, and excellent in matter."

Publishers' Circular.—"We unhesitatingly recommend them to all who can appreciate the ideal of goodness and holiness and the highest form of culture."

Public Opinion.—"These tiny books have much to commend them."

LONDON: JOHN MURRAY, ALBEMARLE STREET, W.

(Please order through your Bookseller)

CPSIA information can be obtained at www.ICGtesting.com
Printed in the USA
LVOW071006060713

341454LV00010B/257/A